THE AMERICAN VISION
PAINTINGS 1825-1875

October 8-November 2, 1968

The Public Education Association

The American Vision
All rights reserved by the Public Education Association
Produced by The Lenmore Press, Inc., New York
Designed by Robert Rocchio

THE GALLERIES

M. KNOEDLER AND CO., Inc.
14 East 57th Street
Figure and Still Life

HIRSCHL AND ADLER GALLERIES, Inc.
21 East 67th Street
Genre

PAUL ROSENBERG AND CO.
20 East 79th Street
Landscape

A New American Vision for Schools

America has always had a special vision in education, unique in the world. Yet today we awake to giant inequities in a public school system about which many have become too complacent. It is therefore particularly appropriate for the Public Education Association to sponsor an exhibition at this time with a title which looks both to the past and the future. For if America is to achieve the new educational goal which now lies before it, it will need perspective and faith alike.

Free education available to all children has been an accepted part of our democratic ideal since the Massachusetts Bay Colony passed its first school tax in 1647. Over 100 years ago, with secondary education in Europe and elsewhere still reserved to the elite, we set out to see to it that every American boy, even though he might not become President, could look to free education through the High School, and (in theory, at least) preparation for one of a vast proliferation of State-supported colleges and universities. It has been estimated that, last year, three out of every ten individuals in this country were students, teachers or school administrators: 60 million out of 200 million persons directly involved in a multi-billion dollar industry.

All this was not of course accomplished easily. Here in New York City, for example, the Public Education Association, a private watchdog institution, has for 70 years worked to keep politics out of the schools, to upgrade teaching standards, to broaden curriculum, and to develop special programs for the handicapped, the specially gifted, the economically deprived. It has fought for smaller classes, for health and guidance services—and always and above all, for larger budgets. Aware that the schools will be only as good as the taxpayers want to make them, it has worked for deeper public understanding of school needs, under the slogan THE SCHOOLS ARE EVERYBODY'S BUSINESS.

Today because of the tragic recognition that, in spite of all that has been accomplished, millions of our children are not learning, the schools have indeed become everybody's business. At a time when education has become an essential passport to adequate employment and escape from poverty, we have awakened to the unacceptable discrepancy between the kind of education being offered the child in a middle-class white suburb and the child of a minority race in the largely segregated schools of our Inner Cities.

We must not only devise but apply remedies on a wholesale scale as yet unvisioned if we are to realize the goal which John Dewey phrased for us years ago when he said: "What the best and wisest parent wants for his own child, that must the community want for all its children. Any other ideal for our schools is narrow and unlovely: acted upon, it destroys our democracy."

Over the years, the Public Education Association has been fortunate in having among its Trustees women whose dedication to the cause of better schools was matched by their knowledge of art. Support of the Association by its membership has been supplemented in a vital way by the distinguished exhibitions which Mrs. Samuel A. Lewisohn, and later Mrs. Victor W. Ganz and her devoted co-workers, have arranged for its benefit.

We look forward at this time with renewed strength to engaging in this next great and hitherto unheard-of adventure for education—the attempt not merely to make education available to all children, but to educate all children.

Mrs. Alvan L. Barach
Chairman, Board of Trustees

Lenders to the Exhibition

The Trustees of the Public Education Association wish to express their gratitude to the American museums and collectors who have so generously loaned their works of art.

We are indebted to the participating art dealers for their cooperation. Without their constant support such an undertaking would not have been possible.

The Addison Gallery of American Art, Phillips
 Academy, Andover, Massachusetts
The Albany Institute of History and Art
The Albright-Knox Art Gallery, Buffalo
Amherst College, Amherst, Massachusetts
The Art Museum, Princeton University, Princeton
The Brooklyn Museum
The Cincinnati Art Museum
The City Art Museum of St. Louis
The Sterling and Francine Clark Art Institute
 Williamstown, Massachusetts
The Corcoran Gallery of Art, Washington, D.C.
The Detroit Institute of Arts
The Fogg Art Museum, Harvard University,
 Cambridge
The Thomas Jefferson Medical College
 of Philadelphia
The Metropolitan Museum of Art, New York
The Museum of Art, Carnegie Institute, Pittsburgh
The Museum of the City of New York
The Museum of Fine Arts, Boston
The Museum of Art, Rhode Island School of Design,
 Providence
The Montclair Art Museum, Montclair, New Jersey
The National Academy of Design, New York
The Nelson Gallery-Atkins Museum, Kansas City
The Newark Museum
The New York Public Library
The Peabody Museum of Archaeology and
 Ethnology, Harvard University, Cambridge
The Pennsylvania Academy of the Fine Arts,
 Philadelphia
The Philadelphia Museum of Art
The Philbrook Art Center, Tulsa, Oklahoma
The Reading Public Museum and Art Gallery,
 Reading, Pennsylvania
Reynolda House Collection, Winston-Salem,
 North Carolina
The Smith College Museum of Art, Northampton,
 Massachusetts

The Suffolk Museum and Carriage House at
 Stony Brook, Long Island
The Toledo Museum of Art
The Wadsworth Atheneum, Hartford
The Worcester Art Museum
The Yale University Art Gallery, New Haven

Mr. Lee B. Anderson, New York
Miss Amanda K. Berls, New York
The Century Association, New York
Mr. and Mrs. Ferdinand H. Davis, New York
Madeleine Thompson Edmonds, Northampton,
 Massachusetts
Mr. and Mrs. Samuel B. Feld, New York
Mr. and Mrs. Pieter W. Fosburgh, Cherry Plain,
 New York
The Rita and Daniel Fraad Collection,
 Scarsdale, New York
The Honorable and Mrs. Peter H. B. Frelinghuysen,
 Morristown, New Jersey
Mr. Henry Melville Fuller, New York
Mr. and Mrs. Robert C. Graham, New York
Mr. and Mrs. H. John Heinz III, Pittsburgh
IBM Corporation, New York
Dr. Harold H. Lefft, New York
Dr. John J. McDonough, Youngstown, Ohio
Mr. and Mrs. J. William Middendorf II, New York
Mrs. John C. Newington, Greenwich, Connecticut
The Rokeby Collection, Barrytown, New York
Mr. and Mrs. Ernest T. Rosenfeld, New York
Mrs. J. Wright Rumbough, New York
Mr. and Mrs. Theodore E. Stebbins, Jr., Cambridge
Mrs. Vanderbilt Webb, New York
Mrs. Norman B. Woolworth, New York
The Anonymous Lenders

Adelson Galleries, Inc., Boston
Hirschl and Adler Galleries, Inc., New York
M. Knoedler and Co., Inc., New York
The Schweitzer Gallery, New York

Acknowledgements

In 1962 a group of New York art dealers first joined together to present for the Public Education Association a multi-gallery art exhibition. An American Tribute to Picasso, a nine-gallery exhibition held in that year, was followed by a four-gallery American Tribute to Braque following his death in 1964. In 1966 a ten-gallery exhibition, "Seven Decades of Modern Art", paid tribute to P.E.A. on the occasion of its 70th anniversary. To our knowledge there is no city where support of a joint enterprise is given in such a spirit of cooperation. We want to record with great appreciation our debt to this year's participating galleries: Hirschl and Adler Galleries, Inc., M. Knoedler and Co., Inc. and Paul Rosenberg and Co. For the contribution of their galleries during the exhibition period, the transporting and installing of the paintings, the gala parties they give on opening night, and the many demands made on them and their staffs, we are warmly and truly grateful.

"The American Vision" began to take shape with the formation of an Art Advisory Committee consisting of Directors, Associate Directors and Curators of the City's major museums. Mrs. Mildred Baker, Mr. Thomas W. Buechner, Mr. Lloyd Goodrich, Mr. John Gordon, Mr. John K. Howat, Mr. Ralph Miller and Mr. Theodore Rousseau have supported the project in countless ways and have been most generous in making works of art from their respective museums available to us. Their unanimous choice of Mr. Stuart P. Feld to organize the exhibition was a brilliant one.

Mr. Feld, formerly Associate Curator in charge of the Department of American Paintings and Sculpture at the Metropolitan Museum of Art, New York, now a member of the firm of Hirschl and Adler, has made a contribution to P.E.A. of inestimable value. Our debt to him for The American Vision is a very great one. His erudition and the enormous amount of time he has devoted to selecting the paintings and organizing the catalogue make it difficult, indeed, to record the measure of our gratitude. It has been an enriching and happy experience to have worked with him.

The introductory essays to the four sections of the catalogue are a contribution, by their authors, both to this exhibition and to the P.E.A. We are very grateful to Mr. William H. Gerdts, Associate Professor of Art and Gallery Director, University of Maryland; Mr. Francis S. Grubar, Associate Professor of Art History, George Washington University; Mr. Richard McLanathan, Art Consultant and author, and Barbara Novak O'Doherty, Associate Professor of Art History, Barnard College.

While Mr. Perry Rathbone, Director of the Museum of Fine Arts, Boston, was not a member of our purely local Art Advisory Committee, we want to acknowledge our appreciation of his interest in the project and of the large number of loans he made available from the Museum's collection. For help in locating paintings and obtaining loans we are indebted to Mr. Bowden Broadwater, Mr. Herbert Brownell, Mr. Charles Chetham, Mr. Charles D. Childs, Mr. Bartlett H. Hayes, Jr., Mrs. Hannah J. Howell, Mr. Norman Hirschl, Mr. Porter McCray, Mr. John Richardson and Mr. Bethuel M. Webster.

Many volunteers have given hours of time to organizing various aspects of this benefit. We want to thank, in particular, Mrs. Lynn Carrick, Mrs. William S. Connell and Mrs. Irving Moskovitz for invaluable help. Maxine Bacon has, once again, been the most gracious and efficient of secretaries.

We would like to thank Mr. and Mrs. Samuel B. Feld, Mr. and Mrs. Daniel Fraad and an anonymous lender for the generosity which made it possible to reproduce their works in color. So many people have given assistance that it is impossible to acknowledge them all. However we would especially like to thank Governor and Mrs. Averell Harriman, Miss Cecily Langdale, Miss Margaret Larsen of Bell and Stanton, and Mr. Nathan Rabin.

Mrs. Frederick E. Donaldson   Mrs. Victor W. Ganz   Mrs. John H. Loeb

American Painting 1825-1875

During the past quarter century—the years since the Second World War—considerable attention has been focused on American art of the past. One artist after another has been rediscovered, restudied, and reevaluated, with the result that a vast body of material that lay unknown and unappreciated for many years has once again been brought to public attention. No era in the history of American art has been more dramatically revived, more carefully reviewed, and more fully praised than the middle years of the nineteenth century. For this period—roughly 1825 to 1875—which was marked by an unprecedented geographic, economic, social, and cultural expansion of the United States, witnessed the emergence of a lively, indigenous artistic tradition that expressed the optimism and courage—to say nothing of the anxiety and naiveté—of a nation quickly taking its place as a world power. Indeed, the 111 pictures that have been selected for this exhibition form an extraordinary visual record of American life and customs during the middle fifty years of the nineteenth century. At just the moment that a national character was being established, American painters, stimulated on the one hand by a wild and picturesque continent and on the other by the bustling mercantile and industrial activities of the cities, were expanding the scope of their attention and were creating a new vision that reflected the growing complexity of life in America.

With few exceptions American painting before 1825 consisted largely of portraits, usually created for the practical purpose of preserving a likeness. This strong portrait tradition continued well into the nineteenth century, until it was eventually weakened by the ever-increasing popularity of photography. More significantly, however, the beginning of this period coincided with a broadening of taste in the fine arts that created, for the first time in America, a demand for still lifes, landscapes, seascapes, and scenes of everyday life. Although a few artists such as Ralph Earl, Francis Guy, William Winstanley, and William Groombridge had shown some interest in painting the American landscape during the closing years of the eighteenth century, it was not until the advent of Thomas Doughty and Thomas Birch and Thomas Cole and the other artists of the so-called Hudson River School that landscape painting became not only an accepted, but a very popular, branch of painting in the United States. Similarly, occasional genre subjects such as John Greenwood's *Ship Captains Carousing at Surinam* (City Art Museum of St. Louis) had been executed in America during the eighteenth century, but it was only in the period beginning about 1825 that genre painting became one of the staples of American art. And still life, rarely seen as an independent art form in the years before 1820, became, under the impetus of the extraordinary Peale family of Philadelphia, a subject that attracted not only a host of specialists, but also one that intrigued such painters as Jasper F. Cropsey, Worthington Whittredge, Thomas Hill, and others whose reputations were made in other fields.

The five decades that roughly define the boundaries of this exhibition were dominated by the hard-edge qualities of Neoclassicism, which was the prevailing mode almost to the middle of the century. About the time of the Civil War the softer effects of the Barbizon School replaced the tight draughtsmanship of the Düsseldorf Academy, thus paving the way for an acceptance of the important innovations made by the French Impressionists in the 1860's and 1870's. There was no sudden stylistic revolution, but roughly by 1875 the character of American painting was swiftly changing. The old order was quickly giving way to the new.

Because of the ever-increasing interest in American art, a number of exhibitions have been organized in recent years to show the development of American painting over a period of nearly three hundred years. The most notable among these were Three Centuries of American Painting, shown at the Metropolitan Museum of Art here in New York in 1965; Past and Present: 250 Years of American Art, held at the Corcoran Gallery of Art in Washington in 1966; and Art of the United States, which was the inaugural exhibition at the new Whitney Museum of American Art in New York later that year. The present show varies from these exhibitions not only in its concentration on a brief fifty-year period, but also in its specific focus on the development of portrait and figure painting, still life painting, genre painting, and landscape painting. Although taken as a whole the exhibition provides a careful analysis of an amazingly productive and profoundly complex period in American art, more importantly the various sections allow us to trace, step by step, the path that American painting took from Rembrandt Peale to Thomas Eakins, from Raphaelle Peale to William M. Harnett, from Henry Sargent to Winslow Homer, and from Thomas Doughty to William Morris Hunt.

This exhibition has been designed to increase the understanding of a very exciting—although still not fully understood—period in the history of American painting. It was a period that saw the emergence of many of our most important artists, including Thomas Cole, Frederic E. Church, Charles Loring Elliott, George Caleb Bingham, Eastman Johnson, William Sidney Mount, Albert Bierstadt, Thomas Sully, Winslow Homer, Thomas Eakins, and dozens of others who made major contributions to the art of the United States. Despite the undisputed importance of these and other American artists, only a small fraction of them has been subjected to full-scale scholarly monographs and catalogue raisonnés. We know all too little of their stylistic development, their chronology, their sources, and their influences. The authoritative book on Cole, for example, is still a biography published by his friend the Reverend Louis Legrand Noble in 1853! Many other distinguished American painters of the period, including George Henry Hall, Ferdinand Richardt, William Rimmer, and J. G. Brown remain all but unknown except to those who have made a special study of the period. Hopefully, this situation will soon be remedied, as a number of highly qualified art historians have been attracted to the field, and it is encouraging to note that books are now in preparation on such artists as Thomas Cole, Asher B. Durand, Sanford R. Gifford, Worthington Whittredge, and John F. Kensett, all of whom were, incidentally, loosely associated as members of the Hudson River School. But much pioneering research yet remains to be undertaken. Those of us who have organized this exhibition can only hope that it will serve as yet another stimulus to encourage the study and preservation of works of art produced in the United States during a very significant period in its history.

Stuart P. Feld
Hirschl and Adler Galleries, Inc.

New York, July 15, 1968

Figure Painting

M. KNOEDLER AND CO., Inc.

American Portrait and Figure Painting 1825-1875

American painting started with the portrait. At first there were the austere likenesses of Puritan worthies, the works of limners who early showed that grasping for the factual which became a marked tendency in American art. The initial decades of the eighteenth century saw the development of what has been called our first native school of painting in the portraits of the wealthier inhabitants of the Hudson River Valley. The instinct for large-scale design of the anonymous artisans who created them lends strength to their naive adaptations of compositions from engravings after courtly pictures by European masters. At the same time the first figure pieces were being painted in the same area and perhaps by the same artists. Similarly based on engravings, these include a number of lively interpretations of such biblical themes as *The Finding of Moses, The Supper at Emmaus,* or *Esther Before Ahasuerus.*

As the eighteenth century progressed, a number of minor talents came to the Colonies—the major ones had no reason to come since they enjoyed plentiful patronage at home. These included men like Hesselius, Jeremiah Theus, Joseph Blackburn, and John Wollaston, journeyman painters all. Some, like the Scot, John Smibert, stayed on and, inspired by the climate of the New World, developed strengths beyond their initial promise. Others, like Blackburn and Wollaston, returned, while in the meantime native-born artists began to emerge, mostly somewhat pedestrian performers like Joseph Badger and John Greenwood. A pronounced change came when the mysterious and elusive personality of Robert Feke appeared on the scene in the 1740's. In less than a decade, before disappearing with scarcely a trace, he painted a series of portraits which rise far above the stolid provincialism which until then had generally prevailed.

Feke was a John the Baptist to John Singleton Copley, the first great artist this country produced, who shares with Thomas Eakins the honor of being the finest portraitist in our history. After Copley departed for England on the eve of the Revolution, Gilbert Stuart and Charles Willson Peale together led the field of portraiture, which was to remain the dominant art form in America until the birth of landscape painting in the second quarter of the nineteenth century, and the concurrent rediscovery of the charms of everyday life in the emergence of genre painting initiated by such artists as Alvan Fisher and Thomas Birch.

The period with which this exhibition deals—1825-1875—lies between the heights marked by the careers of Copley, Stuart, and Peale on the one hand, and on the other, by the emergence of Eakins as one of the nation's most powerful painters with his completion of the famous *Gross Clinic* in 1875, and the mature development of Albert Pinkham Ryder and Winslow Homer. The most significant work of all three of these men falls in the last quarter of the nineteenth century and the early years of the twentieth. Nevertheless, it is a period in which the various strains and tendencies of American art began to reveal themselves with greater clarity. The pursuit of the real, which was to reach a peak late in the century in the verism of William M. Harnett and John Frederick Peto, remained then as now a major preoccupation. It had informed portraiture in the Colonies from the beginning and rose to heights in both Copley and, a century later, in Eakins, but with psychological overtones, especially in the latter's work, which despite the rigid discipline of objectivity give an added dimension to their art. On a less exalted level it continued in the solidity and sense of emergent individualism of Rembrandt Peale, Samuel F. B. Morse, George Catlin, John Neagle, Charles Cromwell Ingham, Samuel Waldo, and Charles Loring Elliott—to name some of those artists whose works are represented here. One has but to contrast the directness of Henry Inman's *Self-Portrait* of 1834 with the romantic self-consciousness of that of LaFarge, painted in 1859, to sense the profound difference in emphasis and attitude which developed during the intervening years.

The subjective and emotional element, apparent in the LaFarge, which was to culminate in the works of Ryder late in the century and receive renewed and redirected emphasis in our own era, appeared early in Washington Allston's landscapes of mood, and is also present in his portraiture and figure pieces, like *The Evening Hymn,* which are infused with a quiet, elegiac poetry. A more powerful and personal expressionism gives a strange and nightmarish immediacy to the work of William Rimmer. An increase in sentiment, which was later in the century to dissolve into sentimentality, is reflected in such paintings as Cephas Giovanni Thompson's *Spring* and Thomas Sully's charming *Spanish Mantilla,* whose mood suggests that of the disarmingly simple melodies of Stephen Foster, and relates them to the illustrations for the gift books and annuals which became so significant in the development of American taste during the last two decades before the Civil War.

That horrendous event is a watershed, not only in the half century of this exhibition, but also in our entire history, and profoundly influenced the course of American art. The war changed an agricultural and trading nation into an industrialized state, which became a battleground for the ruthless competition of the tycoons whose wealth and power grew out of the change. In reaction to the increasing materialism and political corruption which followed the war, many—like James A. McN. Whistler, Frank Duveneck, Mary Cassatt, and the author Henry James—became expatriates. Others—like Homer, Ryder, and Eakins—withdrew into themselves and pursued a solitary course.

The introduction of the daguerreotype into America before the middle of the century killed off within less than a generation the long vernacular tradition of the village and itinerant artist, and tended to limit portraiture to the larger cities where there were those, rich enough to afford paintings rather than photographs, who wished to be portrayed with a stylishness appropriate to their notions of status, now of increased importance in the rapidly shifting patterns of a fluid and growing society. The precocious George P. A. Healy was one of the most successful of the routine practitioners who appeared to satisfy this demand, though he rarely equalled the attractiveness of his portrait of *Euphemia White Van Renssalaer* included in this exhibition. Generally more impressive are the paintings of William Morris Hunt, whose art was deeply influenced by his association with Jean Francois Millet and others of the Barbizon group in France. But outstanding in this field are the portraits and figure pieces of Eastman Johnson, and the early works of Winslow Homer, both of whom surpassed even Mount and Bingham to become the leading genre painters in our history before Homer turned to the epic theme of man and nature in the New World to produce pictures which rank among the greatest works in American art.

In recent years the art of portraiture has suffered a pronounced decline, and there are many who would deny that the human figure is a proper subject for art. Because of this contemporary climate, a display of individualism and personality such as is afforded by this section of the present exhibition is doubly welcome as a rich record of the American past during a period which assumed so many of the attitudes and directions which were to lead into our uneasy but exciting present.

Richard McLanathan

1.
REMBRANDT PEALE (1778-1860)
Eleanor and Rosalba Peale, 1826
Oil on canvas, 42 x 32½ in.
Lent by The Brooklyn Museum
(A. Augustus Healy Fund)

1

2.
MANUEL JOACHIM deFRANCA (1808-1865)
Matthew Huizinga Messchert, about 1840
Oil on canvas, 34½ x 38⅝ in.
Lent by Dr. Harold H. Lefft, New York

2

3.
SAMUEL F. B. MORSE (1791-1872)
Portrait of Lafayette (The original sketch)
Oil on canvas, 30 x 24⅞ in.
Lent by The New York Public Library
(Astor, Lenox and Tilden Foundations)

4.
HENRY INMAN (1801-1846)
Self-Portrait in Top Hat, about 1831-35
Oil on canvas, 13 x 10¾ in.
Lent by the Pennsylvania Academy of the
Fine Arts, Philadelphia, Pennsylvania

5.
CHARLES CROMWELL INGHAM
(1796-1863)
Margaret Antoinette Babcock, about 1820
Oil on canvas, 36¼ x 28 in.
Lent by The Newark Museum,
Newark, New Jersey

3

4

5

6.
JOHN B. NEAGLE (1796-1865)
John Kintzing Kane, 1828
Oil on canvas, 30⅛ x 25 in.
*Lent by The Art Museum, Princeton
University, Princeton, New Jersey*

6

7.
SAMUEL LOVETT WALDO (1783-1861)
Mrs. John Marshall Gamble, about 1825
Oil on canvas, 30 x 25 in.
*Lent by M. Knoedler and Co., Inc.,
New York*

7

8.
GEORGE CATLIN (1796-1872)
Indian Boy, about 1835
Oil on canvas, 49⅛ x 39½ in.
Lent by the Nelson Gallery-Atkins Museum,
Kansas City, Missouri (Nelson Fund)

9

9.
SAMUEL F. B. MORSE (1791-1872)
Mrs. Richard C. Morse and her Two
Children, about 1835
Oil on wood panel, 30 x 25 in.
Lent by Mrs. J. Wright Rumbough,
New York

10

10.
WASHINGTON ALLSTON (1879-1843)
The Evening Hymn, 1835
Oil on canvas, 25 x 23 in.
Lent by the Montclair Art Museum,
Montclair, New Jersey

11

11.
HENRY INMAN (1801-1846)
Georgiana Buckham and her Mother, 1839
Oil on canvas, 34¼ x 27¼ in.
Lent by the Museum of Fine Arts,
Boston, Massachusetts
(Bequest of Georgiana Buckham Wright)

12.
CEPHAS GIOVANNI THOMPSON
(1809-1888)
Spring, 1838
Oil on canvas, 36 x 28¾ in.
Lent by Madeleine Thompson Edmonds,
Northampton, Massachusetts

13.
THOMAS SULLY (1783-1872)
The Spanish Mantilla, 1840
Oil on canvas, 36¼ x 28 in.
Lent by Dr. John J. McDonough,
Youngstown, Ohio

12

13

14.
FREDERICK R. SPENCER (1806-1875)
Unknown Family Group, 1840
Oil on canvas, 29⅛ x 36⅛ in.
Lent by The Brooklyn Museum, Brooklyn,
New York (Dick S. Ramsay Fund)

15.
JEREMIAH P. HARDY (1800-1888)
Catherine Wheeler Hardy and Her
Daughter, 1842
Oil on canvas, 29¼ x 36 in.
Lent by the Museum of Fine Arts,
Boston (M. and M. Karolik Collection)

16.
GEORGE P. A. HEALY (1813-1894)
Euphemia White Van Renssalaer, 1842
Oil on canvas, 45¾ x 35¼ in.
*Lent by The Metropolitan Museum of Art,
New York (Bequest of Cornelia Cruger, 1923)*

17.
CHARLES LORING ELLIOTT (1812-1868)
Mrs. Thomas Goulding, 1858
Oil on canvas, 34¼ x 27 in.
*Lent by the National Academy of Design,
New York*

17

18.
WILLIAM SIDNEY MOUNT (1807-1868)
The Banjo Player, 1856
Oil on canvas, 36 x 29 in.
*Lent by the Suffolk Museum and Carriage
House at Stony Brook, Long Island,
New York*

18

19

20

19.
JOHN LAFARGE (1835-1910)
Self-Portrait, 1859
Oil on wood panel, 16-1/16 x 11½ in.
*Lent by The Metropolitan Museum of Art,
New York (Samuel D. Lee Fund, 1934)*

20.
THOMAS HICKS (1823-1890)
Edwin Booth as Hamlet, 1864
Oil on canvas, 14 x 10 in.
*Lent by the Adelson Galleries, Inc.,
Boston, Massachusetts*

21.
ROBERT LOFTIN NEWMAN (1827-1912)
The Attack, about 1860
Oil on canvas, 12 x 18 in.
Anonymous loan

21

22.
JAMES A. McN. WHISTLER (1834-1903)
Seated Girl, 1864
Oil on canvas, 10 x 16¼ in.
*Lent by The Rita and Daniel Fraad
Collection, Scarsdale, New York*

23.
THOMAS EAKINS (1844-1916)
Professor Benjamin Howard Rand, 1874
Oil on canvas, 60 x 48 in.
*Lent by the Thomas Jefferson Medical
College of Philadelphia, Philadelphia,
Pennsylvania*

24.
WILLIAM RIMMER (1816-1879)
Lion in the Arena, about 1876
Oil on wood panel, 9½ x 12½ in.
Lent by Reynolda House Collection,
Winston-Salem, North Carolina

25.
WILLIAM MORRIS HUNT (1824-1879)
The Bathers, 1877
Oil on canvas, 24-5/16 x 16⅛ in.
Lent by the Worcester Art Museum,
Worcester, Massachusetts

26.
FRANK DUVENECK (1848-1919)
Sketch for "The Whistling Boy", 1872
Oil on canvas, 22 x 18½ in.
Lent by M. Knoedler and Co., Inc.,
New York

24

25

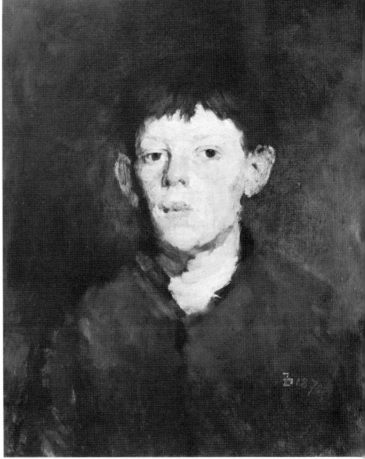

Still Life

M. KNOEDLER AND CO., Inc.

Still-Life Painting in America 1825-1875

Some of the most beautiful paintings created by American artists of the nineteenth century were still lifes, and the history of still-life painting in America is one of the most interesting and varied in the whole range of American art. It may be unique, too, but this judgment must await comparative studies of the development of still-life painting abroad, and the possibilities of influences and inter-action among artists on both sides in the United States and Europe.

The achievements of the Peale family in this field, particularly of James and Raphaelle Peale, are well known. Thanks to the superb research of Alfred Frankenstein concerning William M. Harnett and his school, the story of the most significant, albeit not the only aspect of late nineteenth century still life, is now familiar. Much less studied, much less well known, is the work of those artists who came to the fore in the middle of the century.

It is not surprising that these artists are the least known in nineteenth century American artistic history. The mid-century was until recently ignored or disparaged by art historians as something of an artistic vacuum, between the great achievements of John Singleton Copley, Charles Willson Peale, and Gilbert Stuart on the one hand, and Thomas Eakins, Winslow Homer, Albert Pinkham Ryder, and their expatriate counterparts on the other. At the same time, the traditional evaluation of still-life painting as the least serious and significant form of art, at the bottom of the ladder of aesthetic achievement which included grand manner-, portrait-, figure-, and landscape painting, left the practitioners of this art form virtually unknown and still very little studied. We have even few contemporary records of these artists and only now we are beginning to find their work, see their achievements, and know something about their lives and their superb art.

What I would like to do here is not to attempt in far too small an essay, with still far too little information available, to describe and distinguish each of the major, or at least better-known, painters of this theme, but rather to characterize their collective efforts. While it has been obvious that the pictures of books, musical instruments, guns and game, tobacco and pipes and the like, painted with an amazing emphasis upon deceptive realism, are different from the American still lifes that preceded them, the still-life painting of the mid-century has often been described as simply a continuation of what went before—that being, of course, the art of the Peale family, plus the few known still-life paintings by the Mounts, Elias Metcalf, Thomas Badger, and John Johnston. That is, when it has been described at all, for not very long ago one historian of American art seriously told me that he had come to the conclusion that still life was almost *not* painted in America during the mid-century!

That is, of course, the exact opposite of what actually occurred. The very paucity of names (quantitatively, not qualitatively!) listed above indicates that there were very few painters of still life in the early part of the nineteenth century in this country. And it is true—and it seems inexplicable except perhaps due to the fact that there just were *not* the individuals present with the skill or the interest to practice this art form—that during the early 1840's there *were* very few still lifes painted here. But suddenly, in the mid-1840's, and continually growing thereafter, still life flourished.

It flourished at the very able hands of George Henry Hall of New York and everywhere else, Martin Johnson Heade of Lumberville, Trenton, St. Augustine and Brazil, and George Cochran Lambdin of Philadelphia, the three best-known still-life painters of the day. It was equally well practiced by John F. Francis of all over Pennsylvania and by Severin Roesen of Germany and Williamsport, Pennsylvania, to name two artists more recently rediscovered (the impact of those German artists who came to this country during and because of the 1848 revolution in Europe is a vast subject that demands attention). Superb still-life examples exist by Paul Lacroix, William Mason Brown, Andrew J. H. Way, and literally dozens and dozens of other artists whose continued obscurity is as tantalizing as their art is delightful. And occasional examples of still life exist by some of our leading landscape painters of the time—Jasper F. Cropsey, David Johnson, Sanford R. Gifford, Worthington Whittredge, and others, to indicate that they, at least, respected this theme and would have been as superb specialists in this thematic form as they were in landscape, had they so chosen.

The subject matter of the still lifes of the time was, indeed, not dissimilar to that of the Peales—mostly fruit and flower pictures, with an occasional vegetable and cake picture or depiction of other edibles. The increased size of some of these still lifes, particularly by Francis and Roesen, has of course been noted, along with the incorporation into their pictures of many, sometimes hundreds, of varied objects. This has usually been put down to a Victorian *Horror vacui.*

This is true, but that is not all there is to it. The mid-century still-life specialist was not content with the beautiful austere arrangements of the Peales, with their concentration basically on the formal elements of design, composition, and disposition of light and shade. The later painters shared that scientific concern of the landscape and portrait painters with the specific objects they were painting. They wanted to analyze them completely—to describe the *objects,* in terms of color, texture, weight, volume, and general character. They wanted to get at the "appleness" of the apple, so to speak. Thus, they often presented different varieties of the same fruit, or showed them whole *and* broken open, or from different viewpoints and certainly in contrast with other fruits, or other flowers. The uniqueness of each and every separate object was their goal, and this was a goal best achieved by contrasting these objects—these fruits and these flowers—with others, sometimes hundreds of others.

It is, of course, not coincidence that this approach conjoined comfortably with the optimism of mid-century (that is, pre-Civil War) America. These well-stocked still lifes reflected the comfortable and secure world of America of the time. Although figures were, and are, by definition, *not* a part of still-life painting, the well-laid out luncheon and dessert still lifes of the time suggest the bountiful and the good life. They suggest a contented well-being and the happy family all around the well-stocked table. To reinforce this, just consider the rather dark, i.e., pessimistic tones of the late nineteenth century, and the sometimes drab objects painted then, together with the implications of often solitary activities.

We may marvel at the exoticism of some of the individual floral forms and the combined floral arrangements of some of these painters, but again this scientific curiosity was as much a part of the artists' motivations as was their exotic romanticism. There was no end, not only to God's bounty, but to His variety. And this variety appears even in another way, frankly humorous though undoubtedly unconscious. For, while it must be recognized that this is a generalization, open to many qualifications, pears and apples, for instance, were much more often painted at mid-century, while grapes and peaches were the common fruits early in the century. And, of course, apples and pears are more *irregular* shapes; they allow for far more variation of form than do the globular grapes and peaches. And think of Francis' now well-known predilection for soda crackers. Each one is different, each one has a different character of its own! Or think of the broken, rather than sliced, watermelons—again irregular shapes, emphasizing the meatiness, the distinct nature of the watermelon.

Another aspect of the mid-century aesthetic was the belief in, and insistence upon, "truth to nature", in still life as in all other realms. And this, in turn, particularly in the 1860's, led to an interesting aesthetic phenomenon where the still-life elements were literally returned to their natural settings. The table-top placement was artificial, and rather strange arrangements and juxtapositions were made in the name of natural fidelity where fruits, nuts, and flowers were painted *in* a landscape, and sometimes the objects themselves were not yet "picked" but were still growing—the roses in Lambdin's garden, or the hanging grapes in their arbors. This is why so many times grapes were painted vertically rather than as an horizontal table-top element. It is why, too, the casual, informal depiction of fruit pouring out of straw hats or wicker baskets in a landscape was so popular.

These latter, of course, suggest an action that has happened, a moment in time. And time and change were an important factor to these painters. Rather than the perfection of Raphaelle Peale's fruit, age in the form of spots and other elements of decay, withered leaves, and even an occasional insect that has crawled into the scene were depicted. These all suggest a stopped moment and thus constitute a remote Darwinian connection which was ultimately to culminate in the concentration upon the temporal elements in nature at the end of the century in the work of the Impressionists.

Much more could be written about these artists and their paintings but perhaps enough has been said to indicate that they were men of ideas, which they saw through to a meaningful solution, as well as significant artists whose talents are best illustrated in their beautiful achievements.

William H. Gerdts
Associate Professor of Art
University of Maryland

27.
JAMES PEALE (1749-1831)
Still Life—Fruit, undated
Oil on canvas, 16 x 22 in.
Lent by The Newark Museum,
Newark, New Jersey (Gift of
Dr. and Mrs. Earl Le Roy Wood, 1955)

28.
RAPHAELLE PEALE (1774-1825)
Still Life with Lemons and Sugar,
about 1822
Oil on wood panel, 12 x 15 in.
Lent by The Reading Public Museum
and Art Gallery, Reading, Pennsylvania

29.
Thomas Hill (1829-1908)
Victorian Bouquet and Beacon Hill,
about 1850
Oil on canvas, 27 x 22¼ in.
Anonymous Loan

30.
Severin Roesen (?-about 1871)
Still Life—Flowers, about 1850-55
Oil on canvas, 40 x 50⅜ in.
*Lent by The Metropolitan Museum of Art,
New York (Gift of various donors, 1967)*

29

30

31.
JOHN LaFARGE (1835-1910)
Flowers on a Window Ledge, 1862
Oil on canvas, 24 x 20 in.
*In the collection of The Corcoran Gallery
of Art, Washington, D.C.
(Purchase, Anna E. Clark Fund)*

32.
WORTHINGTON WHITTREDGE (1821-1910)
Apples, 1867
Oil on canvas, 15¼ x 11¾ in.
*Lent by the Museum of Fine Arts, Boston,
Massachusetts
(M. and M. Karolik Collection)*

33.
JASPER F. CROPSEY (1823-1900)
Hellebore, Iris and Clover, 1851
Oil on academy board mounted on canvas,
10⅝ x 7 in.
*Lent by Mr. and Mrs. Ferdinand H. Davis,
New York*

31

32

33

35

35.
JOHN F. FRANCIS (1810-1855)
Pears, about 1860
Oil on wood panel, 9½ x 10¾ in. (oval)
*Lent by Mr. and Mrs. Ferdinand H. Davis,
New York*

34

34.
ARTHUR FITZWILLIAM TAIT (1819-1905)
Wood Duck, Green Winged Teal and
Bufflehead, 1863
Oil on board, 15¼ x 11½ in.
*Lent by Mr. and Mrs. Pieter W. Fosburgh,
Cherry Plain, New York*

36.
JOHN F. FRANCIS (1810-1855)
Still Life—Grapes in Dish, undated
Oil on canvas, 25 x 30 in.
*Lent by The Newark Museum,
Newark, New Jersey*

36

37

38

37.
GEORGE HENRY HALL (1825-1913)
Watermelon and Pink Perfection, 1866
Oil on canvas, 50 x 40 in.
Anonymous loan

38.
PAUL LaCROIX (active 1858-70)
Still Life, 1866
Oil on canvas, 43 x 33 in.
Anonymous loan

39.
ROBERT S. DUNNING (1829-1905)
Fruit and Wine, 1866
Oil on canvas, 24¼ x 22½ in.
*Lent by Mr. Henry Melville Fuller,
New York*

39

40.
EDWARD A. GOODES (active 1855-88)
Fishbowl Fantasy, 1867
Oil on canvas, 30 x 25⅛ in.
*Lent by Hirschl and Adler Galleries, Inc.,
New York*

41.
GEORGE HENRY HALL (1825-1913)
Still Life, 1868
Oil on canvas, 18 x 14 in.
Anonymous loan

42.
GEORGE J. ROBERTSON (active after 1827)
Branch of Transcendant Crab,
third quarter, 19th century
Oil on canvas, 24 x 19½ in.
Lent by Mr. and Mrs. Samuel B. Feld, New York

43.
MARTIN JOHNSON HEADE (1819-1904)
Magnolias, about 1875
Oil on canvas, 15 x 24 in.
Anonymous loan

44.
MARTIN JOHNSON HEADE (1819-1904)
Orchids, Passion Flowers and
Hummingbird, about 1875-80
Oil on canvas, 20 x 14 in.
*Lent by Mr. and Mrs. Robert C. Graham,
New York*

45.
GEORGE C. LAMBDIN (1830-1896)
Flowers in a Vase, 1875
Oil on canvas, 24 x 20 in.
Anonymous loan

43

44

45

46.
WILLIAM M. HARNETT (1848-1892)
Music and Literature, 1878
Oil on canvas, 24 x 32⅛ in.
*Lent by the Albright-Knox Art Gallery,
Buffalo, New York (Gift of Seymour
H. Knox)*

47.
WILLIAM M. HARNETT (1848-1892)
The New York Herald, 1877
Oil on canvas, 12 x 10 in.
Lent by Miss Amanda K. Berls, New York

Genre

HIRSCHL AND ADLER GALLERIES, Inc.

Genre Painting in America 1825-1875

American taste responded to the impact of a number of dynamic forces which materialized during the first half of the nineteenth century. A receptive attitude toward nature and the challenge of the West, the increasing flow of immigrants and the growth of our cities, the development of industry and commerce, and the political and social realities faced by the young country, provided the catalyst for new outlooks and modes of expression. A rising enthusiasm for the arts, often untutored and aesthetically naive, manifested itself. The circle of collectors and patrons widened. Comments about artists and art activities appeared frequently in the growing number of newspapers and magazines giving impetus to the formation of an early school of art criticism and history. The organization and development of art unions, academies, museums and galleries created directional centers through their exhibitions and training facilities.

One aspect of this consciousness of art and life in America was the development of a lively group of genre painters whose chronological development coincided with that of the landscape school. Few facets of American daily habits escaped the penetrating scrutiny of these artists as they focused their attention on the familiar, ordinary activities of their fellow men in an anecdotal, unpretentious, honest and often sentimental manner.

While lacunae exist, the assemblage of genre paintings in this exhibition provides an excellent perspective visual insight into the major nineteenth-century trends of this school. The earliest example is an intriguing multi-group interior, *The Tea Party,* painted in the 1820's by Henry Sargent of Boston. The stage-box type composition, more complex than usually found in William Sidney Mount's or Richard Caton Woodville's interiors later, the casual arrangement of figures engaged in the amenities of Boston social life, the effective rendition of artificial light and attention to details, make this an early masterpiece of American genre art.

Sargent died in 1845, the year that Woodville left for a six-year period of study in Düsseldorf, where he painted his best-known work, *War News from Mexico,* in 1848. Influenced by Mount, Alfred Jacob Miller, and seventeenth-century Dutch and Flemish masters, Woodville was able to profit further by his exposure to European professionalism, developing an impeccable, precise manner which he succeeded in blending successfully with indigenous American themes. The credibility and intimacy of individual characterizations in these paintings is increased when one realizes that it was common practice for Woodville and other genre artists to use acquaintances and family members as models in their little dramas.

Another fine product of the combined Düsseldorf, Dutch and Flemish influence was Eastman Johnson represented here by *Catching the Bee* and *At Camp, Spinning Yarns and Whittling.* Johnson's work varied considerably throughout his long career, from the meticulous, high-finish, glossy effects and brownish palette so much in vogue at mid-century, to a more open, expansive and direct manner which sometimes rivalled Thomas Eakins and Winslow Homer.

Robert W. Weir, best known as the Professor of Drawing at West Point from 1834 to 1876, produced some fine landscape and genre pieces, including *The Microscope.* James G. Clonney's efforts are perhaps less satisfying, relying on overly-sentimental interpretations which are technically less interesting than the first rank of our genre artists (see *The Happy Moment*). A remarkable personality within this group was John Carlin, a deaf-mute who was able to rise above his handicap to develop a competent style after studying with John Neagle of Philadelphia and Paul Delaroche in Paris (see *After a Long Cruise*). He had some talent as a writer as well, perhaps his most poignant work being a poem entitled *The Mute's Lament* which begins, "I move a silent exile on this earth".

Once the westward expansion had entered its final thrust toward the Pacific, our major waterways developed into important avenues of transportation and communication. Life in the river towns was an exuberant, vital affair, judging from the paintings of George Caleb Bingham, the prints of Currier and Ives, and the writing of Mark Twain. The painter of *The Belle Creole at New Orleans* remains unidentified, but his fine style and lively interpretation of the bustling activity of the port city live on in this handsome river piece, which can be dated in the 1840's.

Similar to the subject matter divisions noted in the landscape school, a grouping of specialists in Western genre paintings may be indicated. Some, particularly George Catlin, Alfred Jacob Miller, and John Mix Stanley, took part in exploring or hunting expeditions; others, like Seth Eastman, served in various military capacities. The latter's *Lacrosse Playing Among the Sioux Indians* and *Chippewa Indians Playing Checkers* may lack the atmospheric effects of the work of Albert Bierstadt, but there is a strength and honesty in the rendition of the figures. A West Point graduate who served with the Army throughout the West, Eastman was brevetted a Brigadier General after his retirement in the 1860's and devoted the remainder of his life to painting a series of Western forts and Indian scenes for the U.S. Capitol in Washington, D.C.

Hunting, fishing, and animal scenes were another popular form of expression reflecting American interests of the period. Sporting scenes by William Ranney and animal depictions by Thomas Hewes Hinckley had a rival in the productions of Arthur Fitzwilliam Tait. Born and trained in England, Tait's conversion to American outdoor life was immediate upon settling here in 1850, and he embarked on a successful and prolific career emphasizing scenes in the Adirondacks, many of which were reproduced in lithographs by Currier and Ives. The two painting examples in this exhibition, *Bear and Young, Long Lake, New York,* and *Wood Duck, Green Winged Teal, and Bufflehead* are good representative examples of his style, which changed little throughout his career.

A gradual shift away from the minute precision, dark tonality, and honest sentimentalism which characterized the early period can be detected among a number of genre artists who worked during the post-Civil War period. Their paintings became more pretentious in scale, often with themes so obviously contrived and emotionally sentimental that the overall effect is one of staged, artificial unreality.

Fortunately, however, others were able to circumvent the negative aspects of later genre and develop a more individual spirit of professional integrity. A few simply carried on, with some modifications, the earlier manner. *The Circus Is Coming,* painted in 1871 by George Caleb Ward, is an incredibly fine example in which the small size, strong composition, and precise brushwork combine to give a thoroughly satisfying effect. Ward was a native of Canada who worked at various times in New York City, apparently with some success. His *Force and Skill,* for example, was sold there in 1880 by Leavitt's for a respectable price. Like Carlin, Ward had some literary ability. Articles by him on outdoor life were published in current magazines.

Two of our finest late nineteenth-century artists who utilized genre elements in much of their work were Thomas Eakins and Winslow Homer. Homer, largely self-taught, saw nature in terms of bold, almost flat juxapositions of fresh color, sometimes harsh in effect but never lacking in vigor and interest, whether in his earlier Civil War themes or later examples such as *The Rustics* and *The Morning Bell* with its dynamic, geometric composition.

Thus far, we have been concerned with those artists whose work is part of the central direction of the nineteenth-century genre movement. Their frank, positive statements of American life, painted more or less realistically with understandable technical competence, met with ready approval and acceptance. This was not as true for a smaller group of adherents who are identified more closely with the development of romanticism, in which personal subjectivity and the projection of an imaginative, poetic mood was of greater significance than the portrayal of surface accuracy.

Deriving much of his inspiration from the legends of Washington Irving, John Quidor (see *The Knickerbocker Kitchen*) evolved a robust, original style in which exaggerated gestures and color are treated with baroque-like swirls. How much Quidor relied on his imaginative powers rather than the world around him is indicated by a contemporary description written by a visitor to his New York studio: "Quidor's rooms were without adornment of any kind; a coat of primitive dust lay undisturbed on the window sills and the mantelpieces, and the floor was checkered and dirty. A long bench and two or three dilapidated chairs composed the furniture of the room. A rudely constructed easel . . . was near one of the north windows . . ."

Closer to the central tendencies of American genre in his thematic approach, David Gilmour Blythe turned a caustic eye on the activities of his fellow citizens of Pittsburgh, rendering them with a powerful, sombre palette and with figures somewhat distorted in a heavy manner. The frenetic crowd in *The Post Office* is portrayed with an acrid humor.

William Page studied with Samuel F. B. Morse at the National Academy and through him was exposed to Washington Allston's preoccupation with the methods of the great Venetian colorists, which Page also studied and experimented with throughout his life. Not always successful in some paintings, he nevertheless caught *The Young Merchants* with deftly applied rich glazes and sensitive highlight passages, creating a luminous, fleeting and atmospheric effect.

Francis S. Grubar
Associate Professor of Art History
The George Washington University

48.
HENRY SARGENT (1770-1845)
The Tea Party, about 1821- 25
Oil on canvas, 64¼ x 52¼ in.
Lent by the Museum of Fine Arts, Boston,
Massachusetts
(Gift of Mrs. Horatio A. Lamb in memory
of Mr. and Mrs. Winthrop Sargent)

49

50

49.
WILLIAM SIDNEY MOUNT (1807-1868)
Farmers Nooning, 1836
Oil on canvas, 20 x 24 in.
Lent by the Suffolk Museum and Carriage House at Stony Brook, Long Island, New York

50.
WILLIAM PAGE (1811-1885)
The Young Merchants, before 1843
Oil on canvas, 42 x 36 in.
Lent by the Pennsylvania Academy of the Fine Arts, Philadelphia, Pennsylvania

51.
GEORGE CALEB BINGHAM (1811-1879)
The Concealed Enemy, 1845
Oil on canvas, 28½ x 35½ in.
Lent by the Peabody Museum of Archeology and Ethnology, Harvard University, Cambridge, Massachusetts

51

5

52.
UNKNOWN ARTIST
The "Belle Creole" at New Orleans,
about 1845-49
Oil on canvas, 48 x 72 in.
*In the collection of The Corcoran Gallery
of Art, Washington, D.C. (Gift of the
Estate of Emily Crane Chadbourne, 1965)*

53.
RICHARD CATON WOODVILLE (1825-1856)
War News from Mexico, about 1846
Oil on canvas, 27 x 24¾ in.
*Lent by the National Academy of Design,
New York*

54.
CHARLES DEAS (1818-1867)
Voyageurs, 1847
Oil on canvas, 31½ x 36½ in.
*Lent by the Rokeby Collection, Barrytown,
New York (Richard Aldrich and others)*
Photograph unavailable at time of
publication

55.
SETH EASTMAN (1808-1875)
Chippewa Indians Playing Checkers,
about 1848
Oil on canvas, 30 x 25 in.
*Lent by Mr. and Mrs. J. William
Middendorf II, New York*

56.
ROBERT WEIR (1803-1889)
The Microscope, 1849
Oil on canvas, 30 x 40 in.
*Lent by the Yale University Art Gallery,
New Haven, Connecticut (John Hill
Morgan, B. A. 1893 and Louise Dann
Funds)*

57.
JAMES G. CLONNEY (1812-1867)
The Happy Moment, 1847
Oil on canvas, 27 x 22 in.
Lent by the Museum of Fine Arts, Boston,
Massachusetts
(M. and M. Karolik Collection)

58.
GEORGE CALEB BINGHAM (1811-1879)
The Wood Boat, 1850
Oil on canvas, 24¾ x 29⅝ in.
Lent by the City Art Museum of
St. Louis, Missouri

57

58

59.
FRANCIS W. EDMONDS (1806-1863)
The Organ Grinder, about 1850
Oil on canvas, 31½ x 41½ in.
Lent by Mr. and Mrs. H. John Heinz III,
Pittsburgh, Pennsylvania

60.
SETH EASTMAN (1808-1875)
Lacrosse Playing Among the Indians, 1851
Oil on canvas, 28-3/16 x 40¾ in.
In the collection of The Corcoran Gallery
of Art, Washington, D.C.
(Gift of William Wilson Corcoran)

61.
THOMAS LE CLEAR (1818-1882)
Buffalo News Boy, 1853
Oil on canvas, 24 x 20 in.
Lent by the Albright-Knox Art Gallery,
Buffalo, New York
(Charlotte A. Watson Fund)

59

61

60

62.
JEROME THOMPSON (1814-1866)
Apple Gathering, 1856
Oil on canvas, 40½ x 50 in.
*Lent by The Brooklyn Museum, Brooklyn,
New York
(Dick S. Ramsay Fund)*

63.
JOHN CARLIN (1813-1891)
After a Long Cruise, 1857
Oil on canvas, 20 x 30 in.
*Lent by The Metropolitan Museum of Art,
New York (Maria DeWitt Jesup Fund,
1949)*

64.
JEREMIAH P. HARDY (1800-1888)
The Hardy Backyard in Bangor, Maine, 1855
Oil on canvas, 30 x 20 in.
Lent by Mr. Lee B. Anderson, New York

62

63

64

65

66

65.
J. G. Brown (1831-1913)
Girl Under a Tree, 1866
Oil on canvas, 18 x 12 in.
Lent by Mr. Lee B. Anderson, New York

66.
David Gilmour Blythe (1815-1865)
Post Office, about 1863
Oil on canvas on board, 24 x 20 in.
Lent by the Museum of Art, Carnegie Institute, Pittsburgh, Pennsylvania

67.
John Quidor (1802-1881)
The Knickerbocker Kitchen, 1865
Oil on canvas, 27 x 34 in.
Lent by the Addison Gallery of American Art, Phillips Academy, Andover, Massachusetts

67

68

68.
WINSLOW HOMER (1836-1910)
The Morning Bell, about 1866
Oil on canvas, 24 x 38¼ in.
*Lent by the Yale University Art Gallery,
New Haven, Connecticut (Gift of Stephen
Carlton Clark, B. A. 1903)*

69.
WINSLOW HOMER (1836-1910)
The Bridle Path, 1868
Oil on canvas, 24 x 38 in.
*Lent by the Sterling and Francine Clark
Art Institute, Williamstown, Massachusetts*

70.
WINSLOW HOMER (1836-1910)
The Rustics, 1874
Oil on canvas, 15½ x 22½ in.
*Lent by Mrs. Norman B. Woolworth,
New York*

69

70

71.
ARTHUR FITZWILLIAM TAIT (1819-1905)
Bear and Young, Long Lake, New York,
1871
Oil on canvas, 14 x 23¾ in.
Lent by The Schweitzer Gallery, New York

72.
CHARLES CALEB WARD (about 1831-1896)
Force and Skill, 1869
Oil on canvas, 12 x 10 in.
*Lent by Mr. Henry Melville Fuller,
New York*

73.
CHARLES CALEB WARD (about 1831-1896)
The Circus is Coming, 1871
Oil on panel, 9½ x 7½ in.
*Lent by The Metropolitan Museum of Art,
New York (Bequest of Susan Vanderpoel
Clark, 1967)*

74.
EASTMAN JOHNSON (1824-1906)
t Camp: Spinning Yarns and Whittling,
bout 1865-70
Oil on academy board, 19 x 23 in.
ent by Mr. and Mrs. J. William
Middendorf II, New York

75.
WINSLOW HOMER (1836-1910)
Children on the Beach, about 1873
Oil on canvas, 12¾ x 16¾ in.
ent by Mrs. Norman B. Woolworth,
New York

76.
EASTMAN JOHNSON (1824-1906)
Catching the Bee, 1872
Oil on canvas, 22 x 13¾ in.
ent by The Newark Museum,
Newark, New Jersey

74

75

76

77.
THOMAS EAKINS (1844-1916)
Starting Out After Rail, 1874
Oil on canvas, 24 x 20 in.
Lent by the Museum of Fine Arts, Boston,
Massachusetts (Charles Henry Hayden
Collection)

78.
THOMAS EAKINS (1844-1916)
The Fairman Rogers Four-in-hand, 1879
Oil on canvas, 24 x 36 in.
Lent by the Philadelphia Museum of Art,
Philadelphia, Pennsylvania

77

Landscape

PAUL ROSENBERG AND CO.

Landscape Painting in America 1825-187

In 1867, a visitor to the Paris Exposition remarked:

> "The American collection, as a whole, attracts attention, and has been very highly
> praised by the first artists of France. . . . Every nation thinks that it can paint land-
> scape better than its neighbor; but it is not every nation that goes about the task in a
> way peculiar to itself. No one is likely to mistake an American landscape for the land-
> scape of any other country. It bears its nationality upon its face smilingly."

The anonymous visitor, whose words were recorded in the same year by Henry T. Tuckerma
in his *Book of the Artists,* singled out especially the works of Frederic E. Church for "the for
and accuracy of a peculiar mode of observation, and . . . a manner of composition which is qui
free from the consideration of schools." Thus, our unknown critic offered us contempora
observations which are just as relevant today. It is, in fact, rather hard to improve on h
comments, but perhaps we can elaborate on them. For, by 1867, landscape painting in Ameri
had become, as James Jackson Jarves noted three years earlier, "the thoroughly American bran
of painting, based upon the facts and tastes of the country and people."

Those facts and taste had, from about 1825 on, invested the landscape with a wide spectrum
attitudes, creating a certain iconography of landscape that we have to learn to read. In Americ
landscape was a loaded subject, and in fact constituted a Holy Book in which readings we
prescribed and ways of perceiving identified and classified. The esthetic discussions of the mi
century were more than esthetic discussions; they could be seen as dialogues conducted und
the disguise of landscape about man's place and thus his function in the world.

Every man was expected to be conversant with the Book of Nature. When looking at landscap
painting, his point of reference was a reality that he had to have experienced and prob
according to his capacity. Ideas about Nature, Deity, and Nationalism, the trinity of landscap
religion in nineteenth-century America, were discovered by him in the landscape, so that *looki*
at landscape was a civilizing act—and constituted the critical system he brought to art.

Within this system, the single God acted through many agents. Thus, nature itself, Emerso
wrote, was the organ through which the universal spirit spoke to the individual and strove
lead the individual back to it. The artist, too, was a divine organ, a much more moral age
to express "a thought which to him is good" than were his divine Renaissance predecessors. Th
morality, in its own way, not only dominated critics and patrons, but frequently became
restrictive force for the artist as well. He must neither record so faithfully that he neglected h
divine gift, nor transgress through alteration God's natural works, yet he was obliged, non
theless, to offer up images of mountains and oceans, forests and rivers which would touch th
spectators with the same emotions as "the perception of intellectual truth and the contemplatic
of virtuous deeds".

Given these restrictions, one can be grateful that the artist did not have to contend too mu
with the "consideration of schools". The freedom from convention and empirical freshness
observation sensed by the critic at the Paris Exposition were genuinely exercised by a grou
of American artists working prior to the Civil War who created what we might now perceive as
"golden age" of landscape painting.

With our present perspective, however, we can recognize a bit more readily when composition
conventions from Claude and reminiscences of eighteenth century picturesque enter in. For,
some extent, Claude and nature were still, for some critics and artists, synonymous. Yet, as o
knowledge of nineteenth century American landscape painting expands, such conventions see
more restricted to the "official" art of the time. Though they have in the past constituted th

image we had constructed of American landscape painting, that image proves increasingly questionable.

It is being replaced by an awareness of the direct pragmatism of the American confrontation with nature, a pragmatism which formed new solutions to the problems of light, space, time, and climate with which their European contemporaries were also struggling. In America, those solutions were largely contingent on the immanence of deity. Thus, as might be expected, light and space often became, for the American artist, actual as well as formal metaphors for spirit, and a poetic or lyric response to the plein-air experience was more frequent than an analytical one. Respect for God's nature, too, often engendered in the artists a kind of minute consideration for the small fact, for those tiny leaves or pebbles which, within the context of the nineteenth-century meaning, were also vessels for spirit.

Through it all, a mode of conceptual control gradually emerges as a key point of distinction from the developing optical realism of France—a governing mental process in which the face of nature seems more often to have moved the artist to communion through meditation rather than actual painting. The painting often came later, as part of synthesis, through recollection based on quick pencil annotations. Thus time, too, held in the mind's eye, achieved an extra dimension of eternal stasis, and often became one more component within an American classicism in which control of time and place offered urgent imprimatures of measurable Truth.

The paintings in the present exhibition make it clear that Truth and Beauty were discovered by nineteenth century landscapists through a variety of means, and were themselves subject to varied interpretation. At times, landscape became a kind of history painting, a discovery of the venerable in nature, contributing to a sore need for a national past (Albert Bierstadt's *Rocky Mountains, Lander's Peak*). On occasion, American artists felt motivated to record the monuments of other cultures, perhaps as a kind of annexation of tradition to a nation often pained by its lack (Thomas Cole's *Interior of the Coliseum,* Sanford R. Gifford's *The Acropolis,* Jasper F. Cropsey's *Bridge at Tivoli*).

Tradition could be annexed not only through the European sites, but through European formal conventions—the Claudian compositional formula applied with distinctive nuances by Bierstadt, Louis Remy Mignot, Cole, Thomas Doughty and Cropsey. Those nuances included a unique awareness of the transcendent properties of light as spirit. What strikes one is the complexity of invention with which even borrowed conventions were converted to American use. For ultimately, quite apart from the recourse to certain traditional formulae, the pragmatic encounter of the American artist with the American landscape resulted in the *invention* of a spectrum of landscape modes that answered the needs posited by our culture.

On occasion those needs brought forth (as in John F. Kensett's *Niagara Falls* and Worthington Whittredge's *The Old Hunting Grounds*) objective responses to the plein-air experience that paralleled the proto-Impressionist developments abroad. More often, a more mythical and mystical art was produced in which light, sky, space, reflections, time, found formal and structural counterparts for the readings of the Holy Book of landscape as nineteenth century Americans translated it. The solutions by Martin Johnson Heade, Fitz Hugh Lane, William Stanley Haseltine, James E. Buttersworth, by Kensett (in *Passing Off of the Storm*), and Frederic E. Church (in *Beacon Off Mt. Desert*) all point to the development of an art in which affinities are established, not so much through influence or progression, as through an empirical community of experience and resolution. Fluctuating between matter and spirit, the readings of the Holy Book sometimes polarized, more often synthesized, to produce an art that we, as observers a century later, are just beginning to understand. But we can agree with that unknown critic of 1863 that it was "peculiar to itself".

Barbara Novak O'Doherty
Associate Professor of Art History
Barnard College

79

79.
THOMAS COLE (1801-1848)
Monte Video, Summer Home of Daniel
Wadsworth, Avon, Connecticut, 1828
Oil on wood panel, 19¾ x 26 in.
*Lent by the Wadsworth Atheneum,
Hartford, Connecticut (Bequest of
Daniel Wadsworth)*

80.
THOMAS COLE (1801-1848)
Interior of the Coliseum, about 1832
Oil on canvas, 10 x 18 in.
*Lent by The Albany Institute of History
and Art, Albany, New York*

80

81.
THOMAS BIRCH (1779-1851)
View of the Harbor of Philadelphia from
the Delaware River, about 1835-40
Oil on canvas, 20 x 30¼ in.
*Lent by The Newark Museum,
Newark, New Jersey*

82.
THOMAS DOUGHTY (1793-1856)
In the Catskills, 1836
Oil on canvas, 30¼ x 42¼ in.
*Lent by the Addison Gallery of American
Art, Phillips Academy, Andover,
Massachusetts*

81

82

83.
THOMAS THOMPSON (1776-1852)
New York Harbor and Governor's Island,
about 1848
Oil on canvas, 18½ x 77½ in.
Lent by the Museum of the City of
New York

84.
ROBERT W. SALMON (about 1775 to
about 1844)
Rainsford's Island, Boston Harbor,
about 1840
Oil on wood panel, 16½ x 24¼ in.
Lent by the Museum of Fine Arts,
Boston, Massachusetts
(M. and M. Karolik Collection)

85.
JAMES E. BUTTERSWORTH (1817-1894)
The Yacht America Leaving Boston Harbor
for England, undated
Oil on canvas, 20 x 30 in.
Lent by the Museum of Art, Rhode Island
School of Design, Providence, Rhode
Island (Jesse Metcalf Fund)

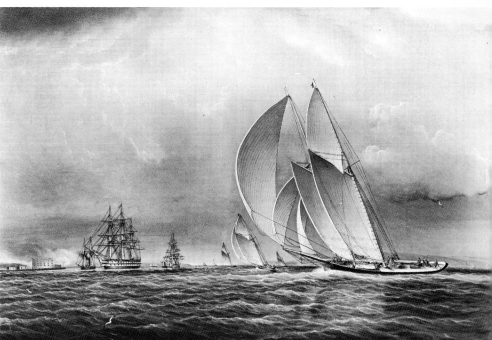

86

87

86.
JASPER F. CROPSEY (1823-1900)
Bridge at Tivoli, 1848
Oil on canvas, 27 x 43 in.
Lent by Mrs. John C. Newington,
Greenwich, Connecticut

87.
GEORGE H. DURRIE (1820-1863)
Sleighing in Winter, about 1855-60
Oil on canvas, 22 x 30 in.
Lent by Mr .and Mrs. Peter H. B.
Frelinghuysen, Morristown, New Jersey

88.
JOHN F. KENSETT (1816-1872)
Niagara Falls, about 1850
Oil on canvas, 17 x 24½ in.
Lent by Amherst College, Amherst,
Massachusetts

88

90

89

89.
ASHER B. DURAND (1796-1886)
Woodland Interior, about 1850
Oil on canvas, 23½ x 16¾ in.
Lent by the Smith College Museum of Art,
Northampton, Massachusetts

90.
ROBERT S. DUNCANSON (1817-1872)
Blue Hole, Flood Waters, Little Miami
River, 1851
Oil on canvas, 29¼ x 42¼ in.
Lent by the Cincinnati Art Museum,
Cincinnati, Ohio

91.
FREDERIC E. CHURCH (1826-1900)
Beacon Off Mt. Desert, 1851
Oil on canvas, 31 x 46 in.
Lent by Mrs. Vanderbilt Webb, New York

91

92.
FREDERIC E. CHURCH (1826-1900)
Cotopaxi, 1857
Oil on academy board, 13½ x 22 in.
Anonymous loan

93

93.
GEORGE INNESS (1825-1894)
Delaware Water Gap, 1859
Oil on canvas, 32 x 52 in.
*Lent by the Montclair Art Museum,
Montclair, New Jersey*

94.
FERDINAND RICHARDT (1819-1895)
Harper's Ferry, Virginia, 1858
Oil on canvas, 15½ x 25¼ in.
Lent by the I.B.M. Corporation, New York

94

95.
FITZ HUGH LANE (1804-1865)
Schooners Before Approaching Storm, 1860
Oil on canvas, 23½ x 38 in.
Private collection

96.
MARTIN JOHNSON HEADE (1819-1904)
Approaching Storm, 1868
Oil on canvas, 32⅛ x 54¾ in.
*Lent by Mr. and Mrs. Ernest T. Rosenfeld,
New York*

95

96

97

98

97.
WILLIAM STANLEY HASELTINE
(1835-1900)
Rocks at Nahant, 1863
Oil on canvas, 21¾ x 39¾ in.
Lent by Mr. Henry Melville Fuller,
New York

98.
MARTIN JOHNSON HEADE (1819-1904)
Summer Showers, about 1862-63
Oil on canvas, 13¼ x 26⅜ in.
Lent by The Brooklyn Museum, Brooklyn,
New York (Dick S. Ramsay Fund)

99.
ALBERT BIERSTADT (1830-1902)
The Rocky Mountains, Lander's Peak, 1863
Oil on canvas, 43½ x 35½ in.
*Lent by the Fogg Art Museum, Harvard
University, Cambridge, Massachusetts
(Bequest of Mrs. William Hayes Fogg)*

100.
LOUIS REMY MIGNOT (1831-1870)
Lagoon of the Guiaquil River, 1863
Oil on canvas, 24⅜ x 38 in.
*Lent by The Detroit Institute of Arts,
Detroit, Michigan*

99

100

101

101.
JASPER F. CROPSEY (1823-1900)
Starucca Viaduct, 1865
Oil on canvas, 22⅛ x 36⅜ in.
Lent by the Toledo Museum of Art,
Toledo, Ohio
(Gift of Florence Scott Libbey, 1947)

102.
ALBERT BIERSTADT (1830-1902)
Pines in Winter, about 1870
Oil on paper, 19 x 13¾ in.
Anonymous loan

102

103

104

103.
JOHN F. KENSETT (1816-1872)
Passing Off of the Storm, about 1872
Oil on canvas, 11⅜ x 24¼ in.
Lent by The Metropolitan Museum of Art,
New York (Gift of Thomas Kensett, 1874)

104.
ALFRED T. BRICHER (1837-1908)
Rocks in Surf, about 1870
Oil on canvas, 11¼ x 21½ in.
Lent by Hirschl and Adler Galleries, Inc.,
New York

105.
MARTIN JOHNSON HEADE (1819-1904)
Two Fishermen in the Marsh, at Sunset,
about 1875
Oil on canvas, 15¼ x 30¼ in.
Lent by Mr. and Mrs. Theodore E.
Stebbins, Jr., Cambridge, Massachusetts

106.
WILLIAM MORRIS HUNT (1824-1879)
Sand Bank and Willows, 1877
Oil on canvas, 24 x 42 in.
Lent by The Metropolitan Museum of Art,
New York (Gift of Francis M. Weld, 1938)

105

106

107.
WORTHINGTON WHITTREDGE (1821-1910)
The Old Hunting Grounds, 1864
Oil on canvas, 36½ x 27½ in.
Lent by Reynolda House Collection,
Winston-Salem, North Carolina

108

109

108.
THOMAS MORAN (1837-1926)
Spirit of the Indian, 1869
Oil on canvas, 32 x 48½ in.
*Lent by The Philbrook Art Center,
Tulsa, Oklahoma*

109.
SANFORD R. GIFFORD (1823-1880)
The Acropolis, undated
Oil on canvas, 19 x 34 in.
*Lent by The Century Association,
New York*

110.
WILLIAM HART (1823-1894)
Upland Meadow, 1872
Oil on canvas, 11 x 19½ in.
Lent by Mr. and Mrs. Ferdinand H. Davis,
New York

111.
DAVID JOHNSON (1827-1908)
Harbor Island, Lake George, 1871
Oil on canvas, 16⅜ x 26¼ in.
Lent by Mr. Henry Melville Fuller,
New York

110

111

Photographic credits

Andover Art Studio, Andover, Massachusetts; Brenwasser, New York; Geoffrey Clements, New York; George M. Cushing, Boston; H. Edelstein, New York; Frick Art Reference Library, New York; Helga Photo Studios, Inc., New York; Peter A. Juley & Son, New York; Frank Kelly, Manchester, New Hampshire; Jean Lange; James Matthews, New York; Bob McCormack; Eric Pollitzer, New York; Nathan Rabin, New York; Joseph Szaszsai, Branford, Connecticut; John D. Schiff, New York; Taylor & Dull, New York; Charles Uht, New York; Herbert P. Vose, Boston; A. J. Wyatt, Philadelphia.